KATIE SOUZA

Edited by Frank A. DeCenso Jr.

DESTINY IMAGE PUBLISHERS

Scripture is the authors' own. Please note that Destiny Image's publishing style capitalizes certain pronouns in Scripture that refer to the Father, Son, and Holy Spirit, and may differ from some publishers' styles. Take note that the name satan and related names are not capitalized. We choose not to acknowledge him, even to the point of violating grammatical rules.

DESTINY IMAGE® PUBLISHERS, INC.

P.O. Box 310, Shippensburg, PA 17257-0310

"Speaking to the Purposes of God for this Generation and for the Generations to Come."

This book and all other Destiny Image, Revival Press, Mercy Place, Fresh Bread, Destiny Image Fiction, and Treasure House books are available at Christian bookstores and distributors worldwide.

For a U.S. bookstore nearest you, call 1-800-722-6774.

For more information on international availability, call 717-532-3040.

Reach us on the Internet at www.destinyimage.com.

Digital Edition ISBN: 978-0-7684-1848-4
Trade Paper ISBN: 978-0-7684-1847-7

Originally published in *Hearing and Understanding the Voice of God*, ISBN 978-0-7684-3803-1.

Ascending

Katie Souza

Ascending

For years I focused on being able to hear God's voice accurately. Over a decade ago, I was sent to federal prison to serve a 13-year sentence. During my stay, I daily pressed into developing a relationship with the Lord, reading His word, worshiping, praying, and listening for Him to speak. Oh and speak He did, guiding me with His voice to receive miracles, signs, and wonders right in the middle of my imprisonment!

During that time, I learned a lot about how God speaks. I experienced many triumphs but I also made many mistakes. There were times when I thought I heard from God but I got it wrong. Other times I hit the mark. As I searched the Scriptures for the key to consistency, I found that Jesus only did what He saw the Father doing, which meant I would never fail if I did the same. Everything I touched would prosper because I would be doing the perfect will of God. (See John 14:9-13.)

As I deepened in my relationship with the Lord, He taught me many ways I could position myself to hear and see what the Father was doing. One of the most enlightening things I ever learned was how to ascend into the heavenly realms to receive wisdom directly from God. James says, *"Such "wisdom" does not come down from heaven but is earthly, unspiritual, of the devil... But the wisdom that comes from heaven is first of all pure; then peace-loving, considerate, submissive, full of mercy and good fruit, impartial and sincere"* (James 3:15,17 NIV).

According to James, the wisdom that comes from this terrestrial realm is *"earthly."* What does that mean? When we seek to hear God's voice while physically standing here on this earth, a lot of things can get in the way. The word *earthly* in the *Thayer's Lexicon* speaks of the physical body we live in. We are three-part beings: body, soul, and spirit. When you are born again in Christ Jesus, your spirit man is made instantly perfect. The Bible says that the same Spirit that dwells in Christ dwells in us. Now remember Jesus only did what He saw the Father doing. So the Spirit of Christ living in you has no problem hearing the voice of God.

Your spirit may be perfected upon your born-again experience, but your soul is not. This is why we have a problem hearing the voice of God because we live in this *"earthly"* body. Our spirit lives in the tent of our flesh and our soul. Unfortunately for us, this is the place that the sin nature dwells. In Romans 7:20, 22-23 the apostle Paul said,

> *Now if I do what I do not desire to do, it is no longer I doing it [it is not myself that acts],* ***but the sin [principle] which dwells within me [fixed and operating in my soul]....*** *For I endorse and delight in the Law of God in my inmost self [with my new nature]. But I discern in my bodily members [in the sensitive appetites and wills of the flesh] a different law (rule of action)...* ***making me a prisoner to the law of sin that dwells in my bodily organs [in the sensitive appetites and wills of the flesh].***

Sin dwells in your *"earthly"* tent. This is why we have a hard time discerning the things of the Spirit. The signals coming from the invisible realm have to go through the filter of our corrupt soul and flesh.

Because sin dwells in us, demonic powers also have the legal right to interfere with our ability to clearly hear from God because sin provides an open door for the enemy to block or twist Heaven's revelation.

Remember what James 3:15 said, *"Such 'wisdom' does not come down from heaven but is earthly, unspiritual,* ***of the devil"*** (NIV). The sin residing in us gives the demonic realm legal right to harass us. That harassment can manifest in difficulty and confusion while trying to receive direction from God. Just as God wants to speak to us, so do demons! They want to plant their ideas in our minds in an effort to cause us to follow after their voice instead of the voice of the Father.

As long as our perfected spirit is confined in this earthly tent, we can be subject to these things. However, what would happen if our spirit could rise above these hindrances into the heavenly realms every time we needed direction from God? Listen again to the rest of James chapter 3.

> *But the wisdom that comes from heaven is first of all pure; then peace-loving, considerate, submissive, full of mercy and good fruit, impartial and sincere* (James 3:17 NIV).

The wisdom from Heaven is pure and undefiled. It is untouched by sin. It is not twisted by our flesh or our soul. It is not subject to demonic influence. It is not limited to our own understanding. Heaven contains God's unlimited perfect revelation.

When seeking direction from God, we need to get up off of this earthly plane and out of our earthly tent. We need to ascend into the heavens where

God's perfect answer to every problem is located. Is that Biblical? Can our spirits ascend into Heaven to get the mysteries and secrets of God, or are we bound to this earthly plane until we die?

Well, the Scripture says that we are citizens of Heaven. Philippians 3:20 states, *"But our citizenship is in heaven..."* What does that mean? A citizen is an inhabitant of a city or town, a person entitled to its privileges or franchises. Heaven is our native land. Since we are citizens of Heaven this means we have the right to have everything that is in Heaven.

What's in Heaven? Everything! The presence of God. His wisdom and revelation for any problem. Healing for any disease. Provisions for your every need. All those things, and more, are in Heaven, and because we are citizens of Heaven, it all belongs to us!

That is great news, but I always wondered how to get the stuff that is in Heaven down here to earth. Well, one way is through the supernatural tool of ascending. The word *ascend* means "to climb, or go upward, **to proceed from an inferior to a superior degree, to go toward the source.**"[1] Your source is Heaven. Every answer you need for every problem is there, but you are here on earth right now. In order for you to get up there, where all your provisions are, you need to ascend. You need to climb from this inferior plane up to that superior one. Why do I call this realm of earth the inferior plane? Hebrews 11:3 says that what is seen in this realm was made out of the invisible realm. According to Scripture, our home in Heaven is superior to what we see here. It is our source, where everything we need is contained.

Because we are citizens of Heaven, it means that we can go there anytime we want. The Bible says we have the legal right to do so. Ephesians 2:6 says, *"And God raised us up with Christ and seated us with him in the heavenly realms in Christ Jesus"* (NIV). The word *seated* means "the right of admittance to such a space." The work Jesus did on the cross won for us the legal right to be admitted into the heavens. Because of Christ, we can visit our homeland anytime we want.

How does that work? Your spirit man lives inside of you. If it were to leave, you would die because your spirit is your breath of life. However, in the eternal glory realm of Heaven, there is no time or distance. So, your spirit man can be in you and be seated in the heavenly throne room **at the same time**. That is how Ephesians 2:6 can say that you are already seated in Heaven even though you are still here on earth. Once we can really fathom this mystery, then we can really take hold of everything that is already ours by ascending into Heaven to get it.

Remember, this is one of the main things the tool of ascending can be used for—to bring all the things of Heaven to earth. The Bible actually proves this. Listen to the story in Genesis where Jacob experienced an open Heaven.

> *And he dreamed that there was a ladder set up on the earth, and the top of it reached to heaven; and the angels of God were ascending and descending on it!* (Genesis 28:12)

There above it stood the Lord, and he said:

...I am the LORD, *the God of your father Abraham and the God of Isaac; I will give you and your descendants the land on which you are lying. Your descendants will be like the dust of the earth, and you will spread out to the west and to the east, to the north and to the south. All peoples on earth will be blessed through you and your offspring. I am with you and will watch over you wherever you go, and I will bring you back to this land. I will not leave you until I have done what I have promised you* (Genesis 28:13-15 NIV).

In this story, Jacob sees Heaven open up and a ladder come down to earth. Jacob sees angels ascending and descending on the ladder, while God is at the top of the ladder speaking promises over Jacob. Notice the order in which this Scripture talks about this angelic visitation. It says that the angels were first ascending into Heaven, then they were descending. You would think it would be the other way around. Why do you think they operated in this order?

Hebrews 1:14 says that angels are ministering spirits sent to minister to those who receive salvation. So the angels Jacob saw that day were angels that were already down here on earth ministering to Jacob. The day Jacob saw the ladder the Lord was at the top of it speaking promises over Jacob. Psalms 103:20 says that angels hearken to the voice of the Word of the Lord. When God spoke those promises over Jacob, the angels that were already down here at work did what angels do. They hearkened to the voice of the Lord. When they heard God speaking those promises, they ascended up the ladder to get the stuff in Heaven needed to make those promises come to pass; then they descended back down the ladder to release provisions here!

That is one of the main reasons why we need to ascend: so we can go up into the heavenly realms to retrieve whatever we need to cause God's promises to come to pass and then bring it back down here to earth. This includes going up to get the wisdom we need to handle any situation.

Jesus talked about angels ascending in this particular order! In John 1 Jesus said to Nathanael, "...*I assure you, most solemnly I tell you all, you shall see heaven opened, and the angels of God ascending and descending upon the Son of Man!*" (John 1:51).

There is that strange order again. The angels first ascending into Heaven then descending back down. Why? Again, the job of angels is to minister to us. When Jesus was here on earth, angels attended Him. In Matthew 4:11 it says that at the end of the 40-day fast, angels came to attend Jesus. In Luke 22, when Jesus was preparing for the crucifixion in the Garden of Gethsemane, an angel came to strengthen Him. So, according to Jesus' discussion with Nathanael, when Jesus needed supernatural help, the angels that attended Him would first ascend into Heaven to get what He needed, then descend back to earth to bring it to Him.

The Bible says that angels can ascend to Heaven on our behalf. However, can human beings also ascend? I mean, it is one thing for angels to do it, but what about us?

We as men and women can do it. Does the Bible say this? Yes! The most important example of a man ascending into Heaven is Jesus Himself. When Jesus was here on earth, He came as a man. Philippians 2 says that when Jesus came to earth He shed His divinity to take on the form of a man. He even suffered and died on the cross as a man in total obedience to God. You see, Jesus Christ had to come as a man without sin or He could not be the atoning sacrifice for the rest of humankind.

So Jesus came to earth as a man like us. In John 3, Jesus makes a statement that proves that He would ascend into His native land of Heaven while he was here on earth. Jesus was talking to Nicodemus when He said, *"I have spoken to you of earthly things and you do not believe; how then will you believe if I speak of heavenly things?* ***No one has ever gone into heaven except the one who came from heaven—the Son of Man"*** (John 3:12-13 NIV). In this Scripture, Jesus is talking about ascending and descending. He tells Nicodemus that although He descended from Heaven to earth, **He was also ascended in Heaven while He was on earth.** Ephesians 2:6 says that we are seated in heavenly realms. Christ was the first one to do it! While He was here, His spirit man was operating inside of Him while simultaneously being able to operate in Heaven. Jesus was setting a standard for the rest of humankind to follow.

Being able to ascend into Heaven seems a mystery too impossible for us to fathom. Jesus knew we would have difficulty understanding it at first. That is why He said to Nicodemus, *"I have spoken to you of earthly things and you do not believe; how then will you believe if I speak of heavenly things? No one has ever gone into heaven except the one who came from heaven—the Son of Man"* (John 3:12-13 NIV). The Bible says that Nicodemus was a Pharisee, a leader among the Jews and a teacher of Scripture. Yet, when Jesus shared this heavenly truth with him, he could not comprehend it.

However, just because we can't fully grasp something from Scripture doesn't negate that it is still truth. Jesus said, *"I have still many things to say to you, but you are not able to bear them or to take them upon you or to grasp them now. But when He, the Spirit of Truth (the Truth-giving Spirit) comes, He will guide you into all the Truth (the whole, full Truth)* (John 16:12-13).

In the Kingdom of Heaven, there are deep mysteries. Scripture is full of layers. As we dig into them, the Holy Spirit will reveal to us heavenly things that we could not fathom before. As we search through Scripture, we see that many men in the Bible ascended into their homeland of

Heaven. In the book of Revelation, the apostle John had this experience.

> *After this I looked, and behold, a door standing open in heaven! And the first voice which I had heard addressing me like [the calling of] a war trumpet said, Come up here, and I will show you what must take place in the future. At once I came under the [Holy] Spirit's power, and behold, a throne stood in heaven, with One seated on the throne!* (Revelation 4:1-2)

John was just a man; yet, he ascended into the heavenly realm. Notice that each time someone went up into Heaven, it was so they could have an encounter with God, and so they could receive revelations. Look at all the downloads John received while he was ascended into Heaven. The entire Book of Revelation was written from His experience!

Exodus 24:9-11 is another proof of men ascending into the heavens. The Scripture says that when Israel was at the foot of mount Horab,

> *Moses and Aaron...and the seventy elders of Israel went up and saw the God of Israel. Under His feet was something like a pavement made of sapphire, clear as the sky itself... they saw God, and they ate and drank* (Exodus 24:9-11 NIV).

Moses, Aaron, and the elders of Israel ascended into the throne room of God, and they were just men. Notice that the Scripture says that they ate and drank. This tells me that more than their spirits went up into Heaven, but their bodies ascended also. Are there other Scriptures to substantiate the claim that we can go up into Heaven in more than our physical bodies?

Well, the apostle Paul said we can. Listen to this Scripture from Second Corinthians.

> *True, there is nothing to be gained by it, but [as I am obliged] to boast, I will go on to visions and revelations of the Lord. I know a man in*

> *Christ who fourteen years ago—whether in the body or out of the body I do not know, God knows—was caught up to the third heaven. And I know that this man—whether in the body or away from the body I do not know, God knows—was caught up into paradise, and he heard utterances beyond the power of man to put into words, which man is not permitted to utter...*(2 Corinthians 12:1-4).

Paul says twice *"whether in the body or out of the body I do not know, God knows"* (2 Cor. 12:2-3 NKJV). When something is mentioned twice in Scripture, you need to pay attention to it. According to Paul, human beings can ascend into the heavenly realm both in the spirit and in our physical bodies.

Let me tell you a story. My husband and I live in a small city in the middle of the Arizona desert. There are a lot of dust storms out there. When they happen, the air gets absolutely filled with sand and dirt. If I am outside, I get a massive sinus headache from breathing in the dirt.

Well, one Sunday we were home. We just finished a conference the day before, so we were very tired. It was a nice day with a strong breeze, so we opened all the windows. We decided to rest and take a nap. As I lay down, I ascended into Heaven. As I did, I saw the strangest vision, a profile of my face and a big huge ball of nose hair sticking out my nostrils!

That's all I remember; then I was out. An hour or so later, I woke up to the curtains flapping in the wind. I opened my eyes and the whole room was totally foggy. I reached over to turn on the lamp, and as I did, I saw stuff falling off my arm and off the sheets. When I turned on the light, I realized it was dirt! A major dust storm had risen up while we were asleep. Since we left all the windows open, the air inside was totally filled with dirt and there was a layer of dirt on everything in our house!

So my husband and I jumped up, and for the next 3 hours we vacuumed, swept, and wiped down the entire house. As I was finishing up, I realized I didn't have a severe sinus headache like I normally would from breathing in the dust. I began wondering how that could be since I was breathing in dirt for hours! Right then, God brought back to me the picture I saw as I was ascending up to Heaven, the big ball of nose hair sticking out of my nostrils.

I was so intrigued; I went online to look it up. I found that the main function of nose hair is to keep foreign or unwanted particles from entering the lungs, thus damaging your respiratory system. When I read that, I got really excited. I realized that we were protected from breathing in all that massive amount of dirt that filled the air in our house when I went up to Heaven! As I was putting all this together, I ran into the bathroom, blew my nose, and looked at the Kleenex. There was not a spec of dirt in that Kleenex, which was absolutely impossible considering the dust storm and cleaning. If you have ever been outside during a dust storm, you know that dirt will always go in your nose as you are breathing in the air. But there was not one speck of dirt in mine.

Now what did Paul say? He knew a man who went up into the third heavens, whether in the body or out of the body He did not know. I felt exactly the same way. To this day, I am still not sure whether I only went up in the spirit, because my physical body was not touched by that dirt.

The Bible makes it clear that men ascended into Heaven, and they didn't do it for just a thrill ride. Every time someone went up, they had an encounter with God or they received revelation. When Moses and the elders went up, they got to see the Lord. They got to encounter God, and eat and drink with Him. When John went up, he received Heaven's instruction to give to the seven churches. Plus, he received the download for the whole Book of Revelation. When the man whom Paul was speaking about went up, he heard utterances that were too powerful to put into words, revelation that humankind was not permitted to speak.

We should not look at ascending as some kind of a flighty supernatural high. Ascending is a tool that God has given to help us bring the things of the Kingdom of Heaven here to earth. This includes the wisdom of Heaven that can enable us to solve any problem.

I was on tour in Oklahoma. When I arrived, I could sense there was something going on in the spirit. So instead of trying to use my own reasoning to figure it out, I asked the Lord to take me up. When He took me, I saw a vision of two witches in black hats and caps with their backs to me. They didn't know I was there. One was sitting at the east, the other at the west. When I came out of the vision I asked God what was up with them. I heard Him say, "They travel together."

When I asked our host what she knew about two witches that traveled together, she said the largest witchcraft covens in that state were in that county. She said those covens didn't stay in one place, but they would travel from east to west. When I asked God what to do about it, He said one word to me:

elevate. Right then, I knew He wanted me to ascend.

When I did ascend, I found my spirit man flying through the sky, looking down at a witch who was flying west on a broom. I was above her, so I just saw the back of her head and her back. She was not aware I was there. I saw this for just a few seconds; then, I just commanded her to fall in the name of Jesus. Immediately, she began tumbling out of the sky down to the ground. Then, the same thing happened again. All of a sudden, I was over a witch that was flying east. Again, I commanded her to fall in the name of Jesus. She also tumbled out of the sky to the earth. That week, signs and wonders took place in that area! The people in that county had prayed for years against those covens. Through the tool of ascending, they were defeated in 20 minutes! When you learn how to ascend, the battle against the enemy will be fast and decisive.

Now I am going to give you some simple steps that will help position you to ascend.

If you really want to be able to ascend easily all the time, one of the best things you can do is cultivate an open heaven in your home. What do I mean by that? In Heaven there are doors, windows, and gates that, when opened, allow you access to Heaven so you can easily ascend and descend. Remember what Jesus said in John 1 *"...I assure you, most solemnly I tell you all, you shall see* ***heaven opened,*** *and the angels of God ascending and descending upon the Son of Man!"* (John 1:51). You see, the heavens were opened first; then the angels began to ascend. When the apostle John got taken up to Heaven he said, *"Behold a* ***door standing open*** *in heaven"* (Rev. 4:1 NKJV). John so easily ascended into Heaven because there was first an open door.

One simple way to get those doors to open is with your thanksgiving and praise. Psalms 100 says that we *"enter into His gates with thanksgiving, and into His courts with praise"* (Ps. 100:4

NKJV). When you cultivate a flow of praise, thanksgiving, and worship in your home, it literally opens the heavens. One of the greatest things you can do is spend time every day in focused worship. I carve out daily time to fiercely focus on the Lord. I mean **fiercely** focus. If my mind gets distracted, I bring it back to the Lord immediately. Scripture says that we need to offer a sacrifice of praise. If you will take time to do this, you will carve out an open heaven in your home. This will enable the things of Heaven to flow down into your home and enable you to easily ascend up into the heavens.

The next step that enables you to ascend into the heavens is to wash in the blood of Jesus Christ. Remember Ephesians 2:6 says that we are seated in heavenly realms with Christ. Now listen to the verse that is right before it. Ephesians 2:5 says, *"Even when we were dead in sins, [He] hath quickened us together with Christ, (by grace ye are saved)"* (KJV). You have the right to go into Heaven **because** you are being cleansed of your sin by the atoning work Jesus did on the cross.

We need to be washed of our sin before we ascend the mountain of God. Let me give you an Old Testament example. In Exodus 19, the Israelite people were at the foot of Mount Horab. God called to Moses and told him to sanctify the Israelites because He was going to come down on the mountain to visit the people. As part of God's instructions to prepare the people for this visitation, the Lord told Moses this, *"And you shall* ***set bounds for the people round about,*** *saying, Take heed that you go not up into the mountain or touch the border of it. Whoever touches the mountain shall surely be put to death...The Lord said to Moses,* ***Go down and warn the people, lest they break through to the Lord to gaze and many of them perish"*** (Exod. 19:12, 21 AMP).

The people were so anxious to see the Lord that barriers were erected at the base of the mountain to hold them back, and the people were warned not to cross over them. Why were barriers erected? Because the law, which would enable the people to be washed of their sins, had not been given yet. So if the people ascended up the mountain with their sin all over them, they would perish in the presence of the holiness of God!

After Moses built the barriers that sanctified the people, God came down in all His glory to verbally speak the commandments to the Israelites. Afterward, the Scripture says this,

When the people saw the thunder and lightning and heard the trumpet and saw the mountain in smoke, they trembled with fear. They stayed at a distance and said to Moses, "Speak to us yourself and we will listen. But do not have God speak to us or we will die." Moses said to the people, ***"Do not be afraid. God has come to test you, so that the fear of God will be with you to keep you from sinning." The people remained at a distance, while Moses approached the thick darkness where God was*** (Exodus 20:18-21 NIV).

Do you hear that? The people didn't want to hear the law from God. They couldn't receive it. Moses responded to them by saying ***"Do not be afraid. God has come to test you, so that the fear of God will be with you to keep you from sinning"*** (Exod. 20:20 NIV). Moses understood that their sin was keeping them from ascending up the mountain to be with the Lord. Moses knew that if they didn't receive His commandments and get washed from their sins that separation would continue.

Now listen to what the very next verse says, ***"The people remained at a distance, while Moses approached the thick darkness where God was"*** (Exod.

20:21 NIV). The people were cut off from a supernatural encounter with God because of their sin while Moses, who understood the importance of holiness, ascended into God's presence.

I would advise you to be washed in the blood before you meet with God. If you do this, you will find the barrier which has been erected at the bottom of the mountain will be removed; then you will easily ascend into the presence of God like Moses did.

Now, once you wash, spend some time praying in tongues. Jude 1:20 says, *"But you, beloved, build yourselves up [founded] on your most holy faith [make progress,* ***rise like an edifice higher and***

***higher]**, praying in the Holy Spirit."* As you pray in the Spirit, you will build yourself up; then your spirit man will rise higher and higher toward the heavens. Sometimes I will pray this way for an hour before I try to ascend, especially if I am having a difficult time going up.

Once you wash, then pray in the spirit and you're ready to go up. You can start by making a decree that you have the right to do so. Job 22:28 says, *"You shall also decide and **decree** a **thing**, and it shall be established for you; and the light [of God's favor] shall shine upon your ways."* Before you go up, decree you have the right to go up. You can also decree Philippians 3:20 and Ephesians 2:6 out loud. Remember, you are a citizen of Heaven and you are seated in heavenly realms with Christ. As you are speaking these Scriptures, it will establish your biblical right to ascend into the heavenlies.

Now, as you begin to ascend, you will need to activate your faith. The Bible says that we are able to ascend into the heavens by faith. In Hebrews 11:5 it says,

> *Because of faith Enoch was caught up and transferred to heaven, so that he did not have a glimpse of death; and he was not found, because God had translated him. For even before he was taken to heaven, he received*

> *testimony [still on record] that he had pleased and been satisfactory to God.*

The Scriptures say that without faith it is not possible to please God (see Heb. 11:6). Obviously, Enoch was a man who pleased God because of his faith—so much so that it was his faith which enabled him to ascend into Heaven without first experiencing death.

What else should you do to get ready to go up? You need to know that the Spirit of God living in you will enable you to ascend. When the apostle John ascended into Heaven, a voice said to him,

> *...Come up here, and I will show you what must take place in the future.* ***At once I came under the [Holy] Spirit's power,*** *and behold, a throne stood in heaven, with One seated on the throne!* (Revelation 4:1-2)

It was through the power of the Spirit that John was able to ascend.

Another point is this. You can command your spirit to go up. John's spirit received a command to come up to Heaven. The Bible says you can ascend because of Christ's work on the cross. It will not be out of line for you to command your spirit man to go up just like John's spirit was commanded.

One way you can position yourself physically to go up is to let yourself go into a deep sleep, or what the Bible calls a trance. When I do this, I get really clear visions and hear very clearly. The word *trance* means "a half-conscious state, seemingly between sleeping and waking, in which ability to function voluntarily may be suspended."

In Acts 22, the apostle Paul went into a trance. Scripture says that after Paul received his sight after being knocked of his horse, he fell into a trance. "*When I returned to Jerusalem and was praying at the temple,* ***I fell into a trance and saw the Lord speaking***" (Acts 22:17-18 NIV). Paul went into a trance, a half-conscious state, seemingly between sleeping and waking. During the trance, he saw a very clear vision of the Lord speaking instruction to him. When you allow yourself to be pulled into a trance-like state, it will allow you to see very clearly in the spirit.

In Acts 10 it says that Peter went into a trance. Listen to what happened.

> *The next day as they were still on their way and were approaching the town, Peter went up to the roof of the house to pray, about the sixth hour (noon). But he became very hungry, and wanted something to eat; and while the meal was being prepared a trance came over him,*

and he saw the sky opened and something like a great sheet lowered by the four corners, descending to the earth. It contained all kinds of quadrupeds and wild beasts and creeping things of the earth and birds of the air. And there came a voice to him, saying, Rise up, Peter, kill and eat. But Peter said, No, by no means, Lord; for I have never eaten anything that is common and unhallowed or [ceremonially] unclean. And the voice came to him again a second time, What God has cleansed and pronounced clean, do not you defile and profane by regarding and calling common and unhallowed or unclean. This occurred three times; then immediately the sheet was taken up to heaven (Acts 10:9-16).

Notice that when Peter was in that trance, he saw visions from Heaven, and he heard the voice of the Lord very clearly. When we are in a deep sleep or a trance-like state, our spirits can go up easily and we can see and hear things clearly.

You will know if you are going into a trance because you will feel a heaviness come over you, a strong pull to go to sleep. If you feel that coming on you while you ascend, don't fight it. Take your pillow and lie down.

I like to get up an hour earlier then I normally do so I am still sleepy. I pray in tongues until my mind gets quiet. Then I lie back down and allow myself to go into that deep sleep. I keep my journal next to me so when I start seeing or hearing things, I wake myself up and write it down.

That brings me to my next point. Interact with whatever you see in Heaven. If God takes you up then shows you a friend who is sick, command that individual to become well. If God shows you sin, then put the blood of Jesus on it. If He shows you something that you don't understand, ask Him what it means.

Now before you descend, ask the Lord what He wants you to bring back. Whatever He tells you, grab hold of it by faith, and bring it back. Anything you see in these encounters is yours because the Bible says in Deuteronomy,

> *The secret things belong unto the Lord our God, but the* ***things which are revealed belong to us and to our children forever,*** *that we may do all of the words of this law* (Deuteronomy 29:29).

A few years ago, during the economic recession that hit America, my husband's company closed down. They only booked one job in a year's time. His unemployment ran out, and we were in trouble. Instead of trying to figure out what to do on our own, I asked the Lord to take me up to Heaven so I could get God's wisdom from above. While there, I saw my husband walk over to a safe, open it up, and take out a big diamond. I asked the Lord what I should do with it. He said, "The things revealed to you belong to you." So, by faith, I took that diamond back with me to earth and released it. A week later, my husband got a job worth a quarter of a million dollars!

Endnote

1. *Random House Unabridged Dictionary,* Copyright © 1997, by Random House, Inc.

About Katie Souza

Katie Souza is the founder and president of Expected End Ministries. She has been featured on TBN, 700 Club, God TV, Extreme Prophetic, Sid Roth, and numerous radio shows in the United States. Her powerful testimony of turning captivity into promise has changed the lives of many people around the globe. She is the author of "The Captivity Series: The Key To Your Expected End" which is currently being taught in over 500 prisons around the world. In this season, she is furiously pursuing the light of Jesus to heal the souls of believers everywhere. Come join her in her pursuit and your life will forever be transformed.

Books by Katie Souza

The Key to Your Expected End

Interpreting Dreams and Visions for Your Soul

Soul Decrees

Made in the USA
Middletown, DE
11 June 2024

55629454R00038